illuminate

LIVING WITH CANDLES

AMANDA HAMMOND & TIFFANY MANNING

PHOTOGRAPHY BY NIGEL NOYES

LAUREL
GLEN

DEDICATION

To all those who are on their own personal journey—guard your inner flame

more than any other treasure, for it is the source of all life.

ACKNOWLEDGMENTS

We would like to acknowledge the generous assistance of the following people in the preparation of this book:
The Grigg Family; The Hammond Family; Mosmania; Kookaburra Kiosk; www.treehouse.com.au; Moss River; Britt;
Summers Floral; Ruth McDonald; Vikki Warne; Shirl the flea market queen for her gypsy caravan full of treasures;
and our fluffy friends. Also, to the team at New Holland—Anouska, Kirsti, Nanette, and Monica—and our
brilliant photographers Nigel and Ben—thanks for your wonderful humor, encouragement, and great team spirit.
Thanks to Fiona Grigg for her excellent contacts and dear friendship; and to Sarah, Peta, and Liddy—who have been our
companions on the Personal Journey of life. A special thank you to all the amazing past and present staff at Illuminate—
you guys are stars—and the people who helped us set the world on fire in 1997—Sally Hammond, Scott Windus, and
Sabine Oates. And finally to the dearest people in our hearts—Nicholas, Tundi-Rose, Jama, Shirley Ann, Clifford, and Dora.

Laurel Glen Publishing
An imprint of the Advantage Publishers Group
5880 Oberlin Drive, San Diego, CA 92121-4794
www.advantagebooksonline.com

Copyright © 2001 in text: Tiffany Manning and Amanda Hammond
Copyright © 2001 in photographs: Nigel Noyes
Copyright © 2001 New Holland Publishers (Australia) Pty Ltd

First published in Australia in 2001 by New Holland Publishers

Library of Congress Cataloging-in-Publication Data
Hammond, Amanda.
    Illuminate : living with candles / Amanda Hammond & Tiffany Manning ;
photography by Nigel Noyes
    p. cm.
    ISBN 1-57145-583-3
    1. Candles in interior decoration. I. Manning, Tiffany. II. Noyes, Nigel.

NK2115.5.C35 H36 2001
747'.92--dc21

2001024671

1 2 3 4 5   05 04 03 02 01

Publishing Manager: Anouska Good
Senior Editor: Monica Ban
Designer: Nanette Backhouse
Shoot Coordinator: Kirsti Wright
Production: Janelle Smith
Reproduction: Colour Scan
Printer: Craft Print, Singapore
This book was typeset in Venitian 8.5pt 13pt leading

Safety and Burning Tips
It is of the utmost importance that you use candles responsibly to ensure their
safe use. The following suggestions can help ensure your safe enjoyment of
candles.
1. Remove all packaging before lighting.
2. Place on a protected, heat-resistant, dry surface, away from anything that can
catch fire, and out of reach of children and pets. Use holders designed for the
particular candle style.
3. Trim wick(s) to 1/8 inch before lighting.
4. If smoking occurs, blow candle out. Trim wick(s), remove trimmings, and
relight.
5. Keep the wax pool free of wick trimmings, matches, or any combustible
material. Keep the wick centered.
6. Keep candle out of drafts.
7. Never leave burning candles unattended.
8. Keep burning or hot candle away from body, clothes, and flammable material.
9. Do not touch or move candle while it is lit. Let cool before moving or
relighting.
10. Keep all matches, lighters, and candles out of the reach of children. Teach
everyone in the family the rules of safe candle use to guard against unexpected fire
hazard or personal injuty.

There has been a good deal of recent coverage in the media regarding possible
health issues relating to candles containing lead wicks, and indeed the Consumer
Products Safety Commission is working toward a ban on the use of leaded wicks.
For your safety, always buy candles with pure cotton wicks.

CONTENTS

INTROD

UCTION

FIRE AND LIGHT, TRUTH AND PEACE

For centuries, the lighting of candles has been both a practical necessity and a powerful symbol of inner enlightenment. Indeed, as religions developed over the centuries, candles came to be associated with divinity in many cultures. In addition, candles and fire have been closely linked to seasonal celebrations of the harvest and the home—signifying rebirth and regeneration, light, hope, and harmony.

The first candles were developed by the Ancient Egyptians, who made rushlights by soaking the pithy core of reeds in molten tallow—a fat obtained from sheep or cattle suet. Early Chinese and Japanese candles were made with wax derived from insects and seeds then molded into paper tubes. Wax skimmed from boiling cinnamon was the basis of tapers for temple use in India. Meanwhile South Americans scraped the wax off the wax palm, as well as using other vegetable waxes such as candelilla leaves, candle tree bark, and esperato grass. Further north, Native Americans burned oily fish (candlefish) on sticks to create highly effective torches.

The Romans are credited for developing the first wick, a lamp with a covered oil reservoir and a reed projecting from a channel. Early Roman history contains several references to candles—indeed their candlelit festival held to honor Februa (Mars' mother) was possibly the event that inspired Candlemas, which Roman Catholics celebrate annually on February 2. There are references to candles in both Testaments of the Bible, however these tend to imply more than simple illumination, for example, "I shall light a candle of understanding in thine heart" Apocrypha Esdra 14:25.

The practice of using candles at Catholic mass began during the seventh century

Resin derived from spices, botanicals, and conifers, was employed in early torch making. In addition to the flammable quality of the resins, they contained antibacterial properties—helpful in staving off infectious diseases.

Within the religion of Buddhism, there is a rich history of the symbolic and practical uses of candles and flames. The ancient architecture of temples and pagodas included structural details for candle placement.

A cousin to the candle, incense shares much of its religious and mystical history as a symbol of dedication to the path of enlightenment. Made from similar ingredients, incense burns to ash as it contains no fats or waxes.

where they were carried as part of the procession. However, it was not until the eleventh century that lit candles finally made an appearance on the altar itself. Perhaps this was due to the introduction of a sweeter, more pleasant-smelling fuel—beeswax.

Beeswax was introduced to candle making in the Middle Ages. This new material made from the harvest of honeybees, was a marvelous improvement over tallow. It did not produce a thick smoky flame or emit a vile smell when burned. Instead, beeswax burned clean and pure. The drawback, however, was that for every sixty pounds of honey a hive produced, only one pound of wax was created. Beeswax candles were therefore costly and only the wealthy could afford them. The beeswax itself became such a valued commodity that it was an accepted currency for a church tithe.

By the fourteenth century, candle making was a registered trade. As candles became more widely available, traveling "chandlers" went from door to door making dipped tapers for their customers with either beeswax or tallow. In England both the wax chandlers and the tallow chandlers formed their respective guilds, and competition between the two was fierce. The wax chandlers considered themselves far superior because their business included sales to the church.

Up until the fifteenth century, all candles were dipped. This changed when a Parisian inventor created the first molded candles. From the sixteenth century onward as living standards improved, more and more homes used candlelight. There was an increasing availability of items such as candlesticks, snuffers, and fancy wick trimmers. Common candles were still made from tallow. Chandlery was a flourishing industry, and many governments saw huge profits in the trend. There were state edicts controlling weight, size, and cost. Candles were usually sold by the pound and in bundles of eight, ten, or twelve. In 1709, in an attempt to control the industry, the English Parliament passed a law forbidding the making of candles at home without purchasing a licence and paying tax.

The growth of the whaling industry in the late eighteenth century brought the first

For several hundred years, Tibet traded gold dust, diamonds, tea, and saffron in return for supplies to make candles and incense.

Beeswax began to be used for candle making around the eighth century and was valued for its fragrance and texture.

Since the nineteenth century, paraffin candles have been the simplest, most cost effective, and easy to produce type of candle.

As much a designer object as a source of light, contemporary candles are available in a variety of shapes and colors.

major change in candle making since the Middle Ages, when spermaceti—a wax obtained from the head oil of the sperm whale—became available in large quantities. Like beeswax, the spermaceti wax did not produce a repugnant odor when burned. Spermaceti wax was also harder than tallow and beeswax, and did not soften or bend in the summer heat.

The nineteenth century brought the development of patented candle making machines. In 1834, inventor Joseph Morgan introduced a machine which allowed the continuous production of molded candles by use of a cylinder which featured a movable piston that ejected the candles as they solidified. The next development in candle making occurred in 1850 with the production of paraffin wax made from oil and coal shale. Processed by distilling the residues of crude petroleum, the bluish-white wax was found to burn cleanly with no unpleasant odors. Of greatest significance was its cost—paraffin wax was very economical to produce, making candles available to even the poorest homes. Although it was softer than previous wax types, another newly discovered ingredient—stearic acid—could be added, allowing a hard, durable, and inexpensive candle to be produced.

With the introduction of the light bulb in 1879, candle making declined until late in the twentieth century, when it had an unprecedented renaissance. Today, candles are a symbol of relaxation, celebration, romance, and ceremony. Although no longer necessary as a main source of lighting, candles are now made in every shape and style imaginable and are available from supermarkets and specialty stores around the globe. What is this amazing appeal that has seen candles become, once again, a household staple?

Most of us spend our days in artificially lit offices, battling increasing stress levels and environmental pollution. We arrive home each day with our spirit in dire need of a peaceful sanctuary, a change in mood and light to regroup and unwind. Candles are both a symbol of eternal peace and providers of a physical light which is gentle and

Striking candles add vibrant color and fragrance to the slick interior of this innercity apartment—dramatically transforming the environment from stark to soothing.

soothing. Candles add a warmth, glamour, and magic that no electric light can offer. It is little wonder that at the turn of the new millennium we are seeing a resurgence in the popularity of candles. However, they are far more than just a passing trend. Candles have not only become an essential part of our home décor, but also a key element in the practice of aromatherapy and color therapy to reduce stress.

FRAGRANCES are regarded as great soothers, providing relief from

everyday malaise and environmental stress. The mixture of artificial surroundings, cramped spaces, pollution, and toxic products has an effect on our general well-being. Many candles contain natural oils and scents, such as cedarwood, geranium, basil, bergamot, lavender, rose, and sandalwood, which can be useful to relieve tension. If you are unable to buy candles with the perfumes you need, consider making your own. With candle-making kits available from most craft shops, this is relatively easy to do. To perfume candles, add 30–60 drops of essential oil to 8 oz. (225 g) of candle wax and follow the instructions in your kit. Even if you don't want to make your own candles, a good effect can still be had by placing three drops of essential oil in the wax melted on a candle that has been burning long enough for a pool of wax to form.

Choice of COLOR is important when selecting candles. Warm colors add a sense of cheer to most environments. Red is the color of energy, passion, and life. Considered very lucky in China, red is said to increase the *Chi* or life force. It is a vibrant color and should be used with caution as too much can overstimulate. Red stimulates the senses and, many claim, boosts the immune system. Orange is excellent for personal celebrations that are sentimental or family-orientated. It is a warm and merry color, lifting dull spirits, and encouraging laughter and sharing. For playfulness and creativity select yellow. This is a wonderful, energetic color and should be used in small doses at daytime functions to add a splash of life.

Green is the color of relaxation. Green has the longest vibration on the color wheel and is used to calm people. To make use of this in a celebration, consider using it for a restful holiday event. For example, Christmas decorations are traditionally a combination of red and green, indicating a balance between energy and rest. Green is also associated with the heart chakra in Eastern philosophy, thus increasing the "heart connection" or emotional ties to a celebration or event.

Blue is frequently used for corporate events where it is important to "get the message across." It is also useful when guests do not know one another, as it is the color of communication. Navy blue is best saved for entertaining colleagues, while softer blues should be employed for easing tension at family functions. One of the best colors for a celebration is purple. It has the impact of black, the energy of red, and the communicative clout of blue.

Black is the color of sophistication and is perfect for formal occasions—nothing can compare with its drama and impact. Note however, that it is neutral in terms of energy and will neither drain nor inject your occasion with energy, romance, joy, or fun. White communicates purity, peace, and in some cultures death. Along with black, white can be dramatic but also energetically neutral. This is why white-on-white schemes can sometimes seem cold. Lighting a white candle symbolizes endings and new beginnings.

Illuminate is a source of information and inspiration for living with candles. It is an exploration of the senses—using color, scent, texture, and light. We hope to offer exciting themes that are both imaginative and realistic. Most settings are simple to recreate, using readily available candles and easily found items. At the back of the book there is technical information that the candle enthusiast will find valuable. You will learn about buying, storing, and burning candles, as well as gain an insight into the ingredients, materials, and scents that combine together to build a great candle.

It is important, however, that you use candles responsibly to ensure their safe use. Please remember: never leave a burning candle unattended, and refer to the safety guide on page 4.

CONTE

MPLATE

CONTEMPLATION IS MAKING
TIME AND SPACE

to still the mind and reconnect with our creative, intuitive nature. While logic and rationality are seen as superior in the modern world, it is sometimes challenging to remember that it is really within our deeper, imaginative spirituality that true riches lie. The traditional way of calming the mind is through meditation. For this reason enlightened souls place importance on creating an atmosphere of stillness and peace in order to "switch

off, unwind, and get back in touch."

Inspired by our growing awareness of other religions and cultures, interiors are turning into calmer, almost spiritual havens. Within our own homes, candles can offer a renewed sense of peace, allowing us to transform our mood from tension to tranquility. The flame of a candle is often used as a focal point for all forms of contemplation—purification, mourning, prayer, and soul-searching. In ancient times candles were used to bring the human and transcendental worlds closer together—the ascending smoke was seen symbolically as a vehicle by which prayers could be carried to the deities above.

Incense can also be used with candles when entering a state of contemplation. Incense is a fascinating combination of scent and fire, as burning incense formed from WOODS, WAXES, OILS, GUMS, RESINS, and SPICES can induce a deep relaxating response. Restful aromas will also add a positive influence to a meditative atmosphere. Find deeper, woody scents and experiment with perfumes that are pleasing to you. Perfumes and essential oils are taken into the body via the air we breathe, and the fragrance helps the body to relax, instilling a sense of well-being.

Decide on the colors of the candles you really enjoy or that are significant or symbolic to you. In the East, colors are rich and sensual and promote emotional and physical well-being. Yellow is for the intellect—burning a yellow candle will assist in clear thinking. Green resonates to the heart chakra, which encourages a gentle atmosphere of love. Indigo encourages communication, and violet connects to our spirituality and the divine. Mix prints and textures with warm colors, rounding off the effect with a dash of gold. Buddhist temples are traditionally tapestries of the richest colors and fabrics, GLOWING in TONES of GOLD and AMBER.

17

Collect items that move you or have a history—such as ethnic bowls and exotic throws from flea markets or foreign travels. Hand-woven fabrics, antique embroidery, and traditional rugs can be awe-inspiring when you reflect on the dedication which went into creating each piece.

The containers you select can also influence the effect of an arrangement. Wood is a strong, earthy, natural element—grounding and robust. Brass or copper conjures up a more sacred energy and is the choice of most churches and temples throughout the world. Glass is fragile and cool to touch. Iron conveys a primitive, rustic feeling. Whatever your choice, always be sure the material is fireproof.

When selecting a single candle for meditation, choose a larger, more substantial size with a generous flame. A single candle placed at eye level allows the flame to be seen directly, drawing you into its light, and calming the mind. Simply sitting with a candle can settle your emotions and relieve exhaustion. If you decide to use many candles in a cluster or around the room, tiny twinkling lights work better en masse.

A busy grouping of fine tapers and brass holders creates a center of energy in the middle of the room. Keeping the colors warm and RICH is the key to creating a lush, golden glow that will bounce off the polished surfaces.

A den with a finely tuned sense of the ECLECTIC. The use of spectacularly rich colors combined with the abundance of soft candlelight immediately creates the sense of entering a temple. Everywhere the eye looks there is a feast of beautiful things, from fresh fruit and flower petals, to rich artifacts from the four corners of the world. Everything about this space draws you in and begs to be examined, touched, and considered. The colors invite you to draw breath and linger a while, the sofa is aching to be occupied, and the wafting fragrances are more than enough to take you to another world.

ILLUMINATE · CONTEMPLATE

Reproductions of Buddha's image are created to inspire TRANQUILITY in the beholder. Buddha rests among a temple of candle columns and Chinese lanterns. This corner gives the room a sense of purpose and focus, much like an open fireplace.

The order and balance of the candles is offset by the rose petals in the bowl—a symbolic representation of male and female ENERGIES—or yin and yang. Many oriental traditions believe the presence of both these energies in an environment leads to greater harmony and well-being.

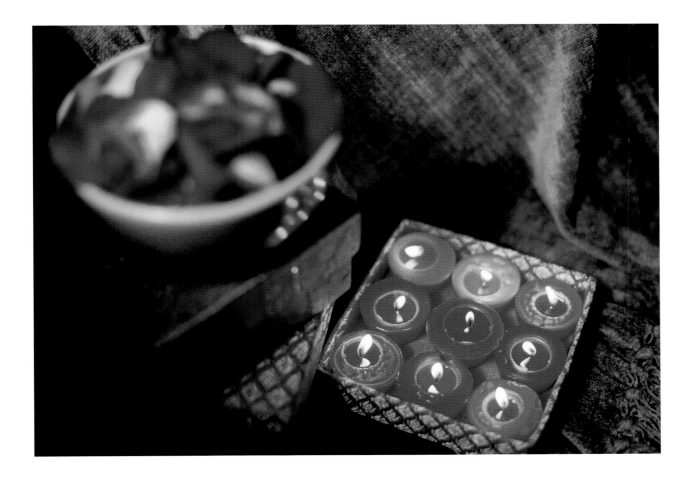

Taking the time to set aside
a contemplation corner is well
worth the effort. It becomes
a place to read, to reflect, or
simply listen to inspiring music
and be lulled by the richness
of the environment. Make an
altar with symbols and pictures as
a tribute to what you hold dear—be it
TREASURES from your
travels, family photographs, or simply
fresh flowers from the garden.

A fully opened fan injects an overall Eastern influence. ORIENTAL mysticism tells us an open fan is auspicious, bringing luck and fertility. Large decorative fans make excellent temporary window displays and, as used here, screen off sharp or dull corners. Candles placed in front of a flameproof fan or design will draw attention to the artwork. A flame placed behind the fan will diffuse the candlelight.

A sense of reverence prevails over this "altar" with teacups lined up before the mirror. The reflection creates a double light and is framed by treasured artifacts from Bali and India. A mirror, such as the one here, a photograph, or even a vase of flowers can adorn your own altar. Ideally, there should be a major focal point creating a backdrop for added weight, then smaller items can be gathered around for color, dimension, and ATMOSPHERE. Experiment with fabrics, textures, and lighting effects. Altars can be laid out horizontally if a mantlepiece or shelf is being employed—or the ceiling and floor can be used for a vertical arrangement.

Tea House Chic. A brilliant glow is RADIATED from these inexpensive Chinese teacups.

A low bench brings candles closer to floor level, creating a MYSTICAL mood. Larger platters with bowls filled with water, floating candles, and petals can be fully appreciated at this height.

Instant wall covering from joss paper can TRANSFORM a back wall and make a welcoming and rich backdrop for bunches of scented roses and tealight candles. Chinese joss paper comes in colorful mixed packets. Select golds and reds, interesting calligraphy, and appealing paper types. Patterns can be placed symmetrically or layered into a collage. Asian newspaper has a similar effect, and is a convincing and inexpensive backdrop to a den concept. Be sure to treat the paper with flame-retardant first, available from any craft store.

Glow with prosperity! These
traditional Chinese New Year
money envelopes make delightful
mini-lanterns for tealights, creating
a soft red glow. When gathered en
masse, together with flowers, fruits,
and VELVETY petals,
they form "Red Dragon" energy,
attracting wealth and abundance.

A tray of scented offerings. Lush
little glasses are filled with beeswax
in EXOTIC fragrances
such as spearmint, sandalwood,
rose, and patchouli.

Balance and form are captured in
an unusual tower of light. A pyramid
of twinkling glasses creates a
GENTLE backdrop. In a
massed display such as this, the tiny
flames are an irresistible invitations to
slow down and take a breath.

32

Use the perforations in the candleholder as a living landscape, casting
shapes and shadows on the walls. Just
as you can be lost in contemplation
for hours over a flame, the flickering
projections from this holder can also be
CAPTIVATING.

Bring added texture to sheer fabric with the use of crystalline beads.
Beautifully embellished fabrics bring an extra dimension to virtually all places
of worship from temples to churches, mosques to synagogues. Riches
represent the wealth of the SPIRIT, so don't hold back. Pay tribute
to all your senses and make sure your retreat is a delight for the soul.

Exotic and ENTICING,
the richness of this room encourages
hours of relaxation and contemplation.
Layer fabrics such as velvets, silken
saris, cottons, and traditional batiks
to develop a tapestry of opulence.
Antique kimonos, bamboo birdcages,
and rich rugs work together to create
a theater for the senses.

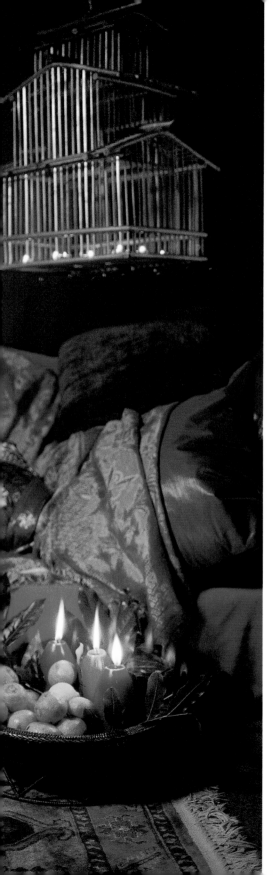

Oversized baskets filled with
OFFERINGS
of scented candles and mandarins
represent the sweetness of life.

As meditators have done for centuries, lose yourself for hours in the flame of a single candle. Take the phone off the hook, seek out MELLOW music, unwind, and go within. Become your own best friend and stop to listen to the intuitive side of your nature. Here a red candle has been set into a bed of fragrant petals and placed on a brass serving dish. This gives height so the flame can be more easily seen. In addition to conventional holders, look for unique ways of presenting a candle display with a slight elevation. For example, by flipping a flat-bottomed bowl upside down you instantly gain extra height.

Adorn your den with authentic but cost-effective junket style lanterns. We shopped for COLORFUL lychee cans. You will also need a hammer, a nail, and a wooden awl to create this effect.

1 Open and empty the can, then thoroughly wash and dry it. Be careful not to tear or rub off the label on the can.

2 Place the awl inside the can and use the hammer and nail to create little holes, allowing the light to shine through. If desired, use a felt pen to mark out your design first.

3 Consider the pattern of the holes. Swirls, words, or, as used here, diamond shapes give a more professional look.

4 A small candle is set inside the can and the finished lantern can be strung to a tree or balcony, or left to sit safely on a side table.

INVIG

ORATE

MENTION THE WORD
"INVIGORATE"

and we conjure up images of hiking through woods and forests, boating on lakes and rivers, or swimming and sailing in the sea. It suggests fresh air and open spaces, being energized and revitalized. The great outdoors can also encompass situations closer to home—the local park, your own garden, and even a patio or balcony for those who live in apartments and city environments.

The outdoors carries the notion of well-being, relaxation, and places that are free from day-to-day pressures—a physical and emotional escape from enclosures and boundaries—a chance to brush away the cobwebs of daily life. There is free time to read and play, to be calmed and cooled after the confines of winter. From early spring to late summer our senses are awakened to the PERFUMES of SEA and GRASS, the tastes of FRESH FRUITS, and the cheers of playful children. This chapter looks at ideas that can enhance your enjoyment of the spring and summer months by taking time to recharge your batteries and finding those pastimes that renew your inner spirit.

Prepare for long summer days. Take your shoes off and walk on the beach. Feel the warm sand under your feet and the sunshine on your face. This is typically a time for lounging, scouting for the perfect spot in the shade, eating alfresco, resting on a colorful throw when the sun goes down, and discovering ways to keep the mosquitos at bay. It is also a time to create magic with candles.

Early evening in the outdoors is when candles come into their own. This is when scents linger in the breeze and the day transforms into a balmy night, with the glow of a candle flame becoming a welcome and romantic night light. Blending the boundaries between indoors and outdoors, daytime and nighttime, is reminiscent of the unhurried pace of carefree summer holidays and all the cues that say unwind, relax, and have fun.

Entertaining during the summer months is often less formal and inspires FRESH FOODS, ZESTY COLORS, and carefree accoutrements to keep the days lazy. As you create props for your outdoor life, keep in mind the function for each object. Think casual, waterproof or rustproof, and low maintenance. Sturdy candles with wide bases, good outdoor wicks, natural mosquito repellent, and uplifting scents, such as lime, lemongrass, and grapefruit, are good choices—as are hurricane lamps and candles in pots that will withstand weather conditions. It is wise to choose candles and accessories that are robust and safe in any breeze or wind.

We are attracted and uplifted by color—much like butterflies and bees—therefore keep your palette close to natural. Think of the uplifting colors of GREEN GRASS, BLUE WATER, and YELLOW DAISIES. Alternatively, add zest by introducing the living colors of madras orange and pink. Whatever your choice, keep it simple, functional, and fuss-free.

Late afternoon and early evening are often the most pleasant and relaxing hours of a summer's day, but can be ruined by the insects that also come out to enjoy the weather. Relish an uninterrupted SIESTA by slinging a light voile canopy over your hammock and lighting mosquito candles to repel these flying insects before they even think about becoming a pest. These candles are citronella free and have sturdy outdoor wicks that withstand a strong breeze. The lush combination of lemongrass, lavender, and lemon work to keep most insects at bay, while providing delightful aromas that take you into a midsummer night's dream.

Move your family living area under an outdoor canopy for the summer. An all-day outing on the beach or by the river can benefit from this good source of shade. Unlike a standard sun umbrella, this awning will accommodate a family or create the ideal venue for an intimate soirée. The rectangular shape marks out the territory for the day and provides a camp—somewhere to unload, spread out a PICNIC, take a nap, read a book, and, for the children, a place to play out of the sun. The design and construction of the awning could not be easier. A length of fabric is lashed to bamboo poles, which are fixed into place with tent pegs. Picnic food is served alfresco on a low table next to large, soft cushions. This creates a mood for lolling around, with lunch extending into the evening hours.

Alfresco dining is the spirit of modern cuisine. Incorporate deep blues or lush greens to dress up daytime lunches, and candles with TROPICAL scents like coconut, frangipani, and passionfruit to evoke a holiday mood. Preparing the table can be a social activity that gives the occasion its vital ingredient—fun! As adults prepare salad, fruit, and pour cool drinks, the children can explore the shore to find "treasures," such as shells and driftwood to decorate the table. Little glasses can be filled with tealights to add a twinkling magic as the sun sets and conversation rolls into the evening. The crowns of the pineapples have become impromptu candleholders with the central spikes plucked away to make room for mini-candles.

47

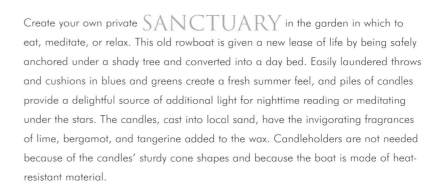

Create your own private SANCTUARY in the garden in which to eat, meditate, or relax. This old rowboat is given a new lease of life by being safely anchored under a shady tree and converted into a day bed. Easily laundered throws and cushions in blues and greens create a fresh summer feel, and piles of candles provide a delightful source of additional light for nighttime reading or meditating under the stars. The candles, cast into local sand, have the invigorating fragrances of lime, bergamot, and tangerine added to the wax. Candleholders are not needed because of the candles' sturdy cone shapes and because the boat is made of heat-resistant material.

Warm summer evenings beckon people outdoors for meals, conversation, or just simply to watch the stars. However, some form of lighting is necessary. Evening is a romantic and peaceful time, and the light should reflect this softness. Although there are a number of outdoor electrical lights available today, undoubtedly the most beautiful and evocative sources of light are candles. Jar candles are easy to make and when strung in trees with wire, TRANSFORM a garden setting into a magical wonderland. This collection is created from assorted glass jars found in the average kitchen.

A trio of hanging wire lanterns set the night sky ABLAZE and create a waterfall of flowing light and wax. For this reason, it is best not to hang these lanterns overhead, but rather to the side of any footpaths where they can be appreciated by passers-by without any mishaps.

These small white paper bags are pre-treated, flame-resistant "luminaria" bags. They are filled with sand, and a small candle was placed inside to make effective, low-level garden lights. When lining a stone wall along a river, they create a boundary and a delightful MOOD.

Nothing could create a more holiday-by-the-sea feel than this driftwood mobile. Use on the beach at night or in an outdoor area to catch the BREEZE. After a hard day's beachcombing, any flame-resistant pieces such as pumice stone, shells, and damp seaweed can be rinsed and tied with fishing line to a support beam of driftwood. Candles are then wired evenly across the beam and the more unusual "treasures," such as feathers, are added to become tails.

54

Here the luminaria bags are given the more formal role of guiding guests to the front door. Scented glass votive candles have been used inside the bags to add a welcoming fragrance. The row of lights begs to be followed and creates a sensually refined entrance as the spectacular showing of SPRING flowers is given a second life after dark.

SEASIDE aromas and scattered shells can recreate a visit to the seaside in an urban terrace. If you have a treasure haul from your latest visit to the ocean, try this. Rinse the shells and leave them to dry. Then sprinkle them with spearmint essential oil. Spread sand thickly over a large tray, and then scatter low candles and the rinsed "treasures" over the sand. If the tray is waterproof and deep enough, water can cover the sand and shells.

For outdoor entertaining, a summer hue has been added to these pool candles by entwining fresh flowers around florist's wire to make bright wreaths. The black candle creates a stunning contrast with the yellow flowers and turquoise WATER. If pool candles are unavailable, try using colorful, lightweight plastic bowls filled with a cup of damp sand and a tealight for a similar effect. The pool candles can be left to float at random or placed within a boundary, such as a light hula-hoop, or tied in a line. If you want a maritime theme, tether floating bowls together with old boat ropes and buoys. For a tropical celebration, use leis and hibiscus flowers to create a colorful centerpiece within the pool. Even in the cooler months, a stunning romantic glow can emanate from the poolside with larger floating candles drifting and bobbing.

For children, both young and old, a birthday by the beach can be very memorable. Here is a solution where everybody gets to build a cake and blow out a candle. This is also a great alternative for someone who has too many candles to fit on a cake, or for those who prefer a more unconventional way to celebrate the occasion. Think of inventive games, such as musical SANDCASTLES, and make group wishes for the guest of honor.

After a row down the river, lazing on a versatile deck chair is an easy way to escape for a few stolen hours. Fill your picnic basket with snacks, novels, and suntan cream for an undisturbed LAZY getaway. Add soft cushions, bright candles, and a crisp bottle of white wine to turn your afternoon into a five-star experience.

Use aspects of the immediate environment to decorate plain candles. Here, large, fresh, green LEAVES from a nearby tree have been wrapped around big lantern candles and then simply tied with twine, creating a lush, exotic look. This idea can be extended to the use of twigs, seaweed, flowers, local grasses, rocks, shells, or bark. Ensure that the candle is one that will form a shell around the edges as it burns down. As this candle burns into itself, the flame will reveal the intricate structure of the leaves.

Attention has been deliberately drawn to this spectacular bird's nest fern by placing a candle in its center. If you have features in your garden, such as rock gardens or flowering shrubs, use candlelight to turn them into a focal point. A circle of candles around the base of a lovely topiary creates a mystical fairyland, as do candles NESTLED into wide branches of big old trees.

For a pure burst of color, this floating candle technique is very effective. Here, oversized sunflowers have been teamed with yellow floating candles in a tank vase for an EXCITING centerpiece. Try large fresh leaves and green floating candles for a more tranquil but equally effective display, or shells in combination with blue floaters for a nautical theme. Fruits, colorful stones, aquarium accessories, brightly colored children's plastic toys, stone sculptures, and even costume jewelery are all items that can kick off a floating candle vase theme.

62

Formal yet funky, this idea requires more work, but it's worth it if you really want to make a SPLASH. Dark blue candles are firmly anchored into glass hurricane lanterns to stop them from floating when the water is added. Purified water is then poured to three-quarters of the way up the candle. Then carefully introduce goldfish. We chose a nondrip candle in a contrast color to the fish. Decorative fish with stripes or spots could have been used, or floating candles as an alternative to the pillar. Remember to give the fish a friendly home after the event!

63

There is nothing easier than
CREATING wax bead
candles from coconuts, sea shells,
pods, and other beach finds. To
create this effect, you will need 3 ft.
(1m) of wick, paraffin beads, and
one packet of tabs to make about
six coconut shells or a dozen oyster
shell candles. These are available
from craft shops.

4

5

1 Clean the meat out of the oyster shells, then wash and dry them thoroughly. If using whole coconuts—split them open with a hammer and chisel, drain the milk, and then dry the flesh with paper towels.

2 Scented oils and wax dyes can be added to the paraffin beads to create a multitude of effects.

3 Cut the wicks to size. The correct size is easily calculated by adding about 1 inch (2.5 cm) to the depth of the item you are filling. Thread onto each wick length a tab, which will act as a foot or base.

4 Set each wick centrally and upright in the shell and carefully fill the shell to the rim with wax beads.

5 Make the most of your garden by illuminating a pretty spot with a flickering candle display made from natural elements.

LUXU

RIATE

LUXURY IS THE ESSENCE

of QUALITY, ABUNDANCE, and PLEASURE.
Those things in life that elevate your senses and whisk you away to another time and place
where the cares of the world cannot reach you. Modern luxury is about feeding the sensual
side of our nature without compromise. It's hand-beaded fabrics, soft cashmere, plush
linen, breakfast in bed, scented candles, fresh fruit, and the smell of freshly-brewed coffee.

It is also those intangible things, such as a long hot bath, a
big hug, or a slow kiss.

Exquisite beauty, pleasure, and peace are all hallmarks
of luxury. Whether purchased or created, introducing
luxury into your home is going one step beyond comfort
and treating yourself like a first-class passenger. Put aside
the mundane belongings that you see or handle on a
day-to-day basis and replace them with your favorite
possessions. Try drinking spring water from your best
crystal, sleeping under sheets that have been perfumed
with your most treasured scent, and gracing your
bedroom with freshly cut flowers.

A cosy bed is the ultimate cocoon. Although sleep is when the body rests and
repairs, bedrooms are a place to do more than snooze. They are places where we nurture
ourselves, dream, love, sleep, nestle, and spend one-third of our lives. The ritual of
"turning down the sheets" at bedtime is the perfect opportunity to prepare the room
before retiring. Scented candles can be given time to fill the room with their dreamy
aroma, and other preparations, such as fluffing up pillows and setting out cool water,
are all thoughtful ways to attend to bedtime. Subtly-scented, low-maintenance candles
are the best choice for a bedroom setting. Votives are ideal when they are contained in
glass. Select perfumed blends that emit deeper woody notes, mellow florals, and mild

spices. CEDARWOOD, NEROLI, and PINE are gentle scents to fall asleep to. For a deeper sedative effect, try bases of clary, sage, vetiver, or sandalwood. Mellow aphrodisiacs include patchouli, ylang ylang, and jasmine.

Good quality votives made from soft wax will turn to liquid after a short period of burning. Once this happens, it is unwise to move the candle around, so bear this in mind when positioning the candle, and find a stable home that is away from flammable soft furnishings. Long burning candles are an alternative. Made from harder waxes, they should provide many hours of light without needing to be replaced. This means they can be incorporated as a semipermanent lighting source, such as a bedside light.

The pure indulgence of a bath is a legitimate excuse to slip away from the stresses of everyday life. Take these stolen moments to meditate and reconnect with your own sense of self. A nice hot bath is both comforting and regenerating, and from a long soak you can emerge reborn. Drawing a bath can be a meditation in itself. While preparing the scented water, select fluffy towels and nightclothes, and listen to your favorite music. Relaxation is your aim so find fragrances that are soothing, such as tangerine, lavender, geranium, and neroli.

Bathroom candles need to be carefully selected as they will be exposed to heat and moisture. Light the candles before running the bath, as the humidity may affect the wicks and prevent lighting. Choose accessories that will not be damaged by the humid conditions and avoid strongly colored candles, as the color may bleed onto ceramic surfaces and stain. As bathrooms tend to be smaller rooms, scale down the size of your candle choice to fit on stable surfaces.

A boudoir of true splendor—
serious sleeping mixed with divine
DECADENCE.
Lair, nest, den...the bedroom is
indeed a sacred space, so create
your own retreat for the senses to
honor this sanctuary. You can add
contemporary grace to the bedroom
by using accessories with textures that
live, from mohair and sheepskin throws
to cotton and suede cushions. Build
layers of textures, shapes, and soothing
shades in carefully chosen fabrics. Turn
your bedroom into the boudoir of a
screen goddess with touches of sensual
luxury, including playful furs and
feathers, sexy silk and satin, pale
chiffon and afghan shag pile. Classic
Hollywood glamour can be achieved
by flattering light and candles offering
a forgiving glow.

Make your bed a PLEASURE zone—move in for the day and bring all the creature comforts with you. Time for tea? Have a stash of treats ready and present them in five-star luxury. Include flowers, fine china, candles, and herbal tea. Tea really does taste better when you drink it from a thin-rimmed cup, so don't forget your best china. Bon appetit!

Frivolous and feminine, a few soft faux feathers from a powder puff have been secured around a glass votive with a diamanté clip. A tiny touch of luxury trim can effortlessly add glamour and SENSUALITY to any bedroom or bathroom.

A flame glowing behind any type of CRYSTAL will shine with an unmistakable sparkle. Like diamonds, they have a unique way of refracting the light—projecting prisms of color across the room. When a chandelier is out of the question translate the concept into something you have on hand. Here we hung crystal beads around the frame of a wire lantern.

A cache of candles forms a boundary between bed and boudoir, providing a playful line to cross. Casting enough light to dress, or indeed undress, candles can be used to frame a scene and add intrigue and ROMANCE to virtually any location. Even a fluffy blanket on the floor can be framed by candles to form a love nest. This row of lilac candles has been nestled into feathers to add a subtle softness to the arrangement. Be sure to use candles that form a wax shell around the edges as they burn down.

Absolute COMFORT without compromise. Curl up in a big armchair and create a refuge. An ideal transition from bath to bed, this is a place to settle and unwind, sip herbal tea, touch up your toenails, read the latest magazine, and share secrets with a diary. Use tranquil colors, soft dim light, and nurturing textures.

The base of this silk flower has been transformed into an extremely pretty candleholder. The petals have been treated with a flame retardant and then scented with damask rose perfume. A fine, ELEGANT nondrip candle is placed in the center. As an alternative, place a small glass votice with tealight in the center. The effect is even more voluptuous with a real rose in full bloom with velvety petals. Float the flower in water for added romance.

Refined texture is the key to creating
LUXURIOUS
surroundings. Here, black raven's
feathers which beg to be stroked are
wrapped around glasses with tealights
placed inside. Feathers of all types
look stunning when illuminated. For a
delightful frou-frou touch, try circling
lengths of feather boas around large
vases and setting the vases with
floating candles.

Poets quite rightly endow
PERFUMES with the
power to create sweet intoxication for
the soul. For bed or bath time, choose
warm floral scents, such as jasmine or
neroli, which are soothing and calming.

A twinkling serenade of tiny
SCENTED candles can
be clustered together on little trays
lined with fire-safe materials.
The charm of massed candles is
evident here, and the light cast has
a delicate, angelic softness.

Creating an enticing pathway to the bedroom or bathroom engages the senses before you even arrive at your destination. It is a tantalizing promise of what is yet to come. Fragrance the journey with DELIGHTS such as honeysuckle, gardenia, and geranium. Placed at this height, the candles will create an upglow, throwing more light than usual into the space. Select nondrip candles and ensure they are placed well away from walls and flammable soft furnishings.

Candles on the dresser offer a light which is both flattering and SEDUCTIVE. Make the most of your time in front of the mirror by pampering yourself silly. Surround yourself with your favorite trinkets. Display everything from diamonds to pearls around the base of candles. This cone shape is ideal, as it won't drip as it burns.

Awaken your senses. Fragrant sachets, scented water, textured bathmats, FLUFFY towels in muted tones, soft music, soapy bubbles, and dreamy perfumes are all heaven-sent for those who want to turn the bathroom into a true sanctuary. Candlelight transforms the bathroom from cold functionality into a private, intimate temple for the senses. Water is symbolic of emotions and the feminine principle, so taking a bath can bring you in touch with your psyche and intuition. By setting the bathroom with candles, you create an atmosphere of sensuality and pleasure—enabling you to take the time to become aware of your body and feel the water against your skin.

Stack, cluster, and store your favorite bath goodies so you can have all your INDULGENCES close at hand. Low basket trays are ideal for this. Line a tray with a soft, light hand towel to absorb moisture and pile up loofahs, sponges, pumice, milks, salts, creams, and, of course, scented candles. Have one basket for the body, one for the feet, and one for the face.

Slip into something spectacular at the end of a long soak. Fluffy slippers, thick towels, and generous bathrobes are essential. Toes can be tickled by ultrashaggy Greek rugs called flokarti. Consider how TEXTURES feel against bare skin when choosing your bathroom accessories. Have a wide easychair in your bathroom so you can linger in the steamy atmosphere—after all, what's the rush?

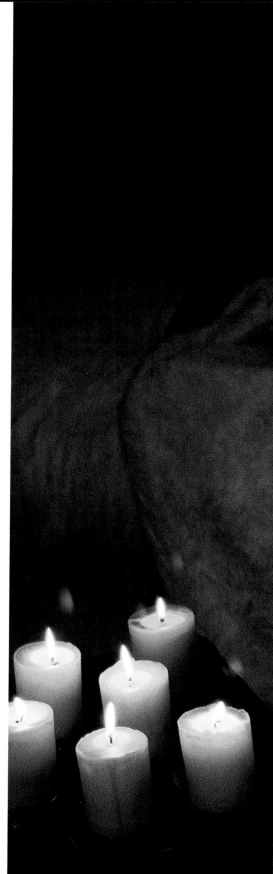

Although Cleopatra seduced Anthony on a bed of roses, lilies are one of nature's most potent aphrodisiacs. Float these GLORIOUS flowers in your bathtub, add a few drops of essential oil to the steamy waters, and surround yourself with candles scented with ylang ylang.

The PERFECT treatment for bottles that are too precious or interesting to toss out: turn them into candleholders or reuse them by decanting products from lackluster packaging. This French fragrant water bottle was embellished with a handmade crystal collar, simply constructed from fine wire and beads.

Create your own soap opera! A humble soap dish has become a cheeky accessory with the addition of drop JEWELS and some perky tealights. Hunt around for unusual soap dishes, as they can make terrific candleholders.

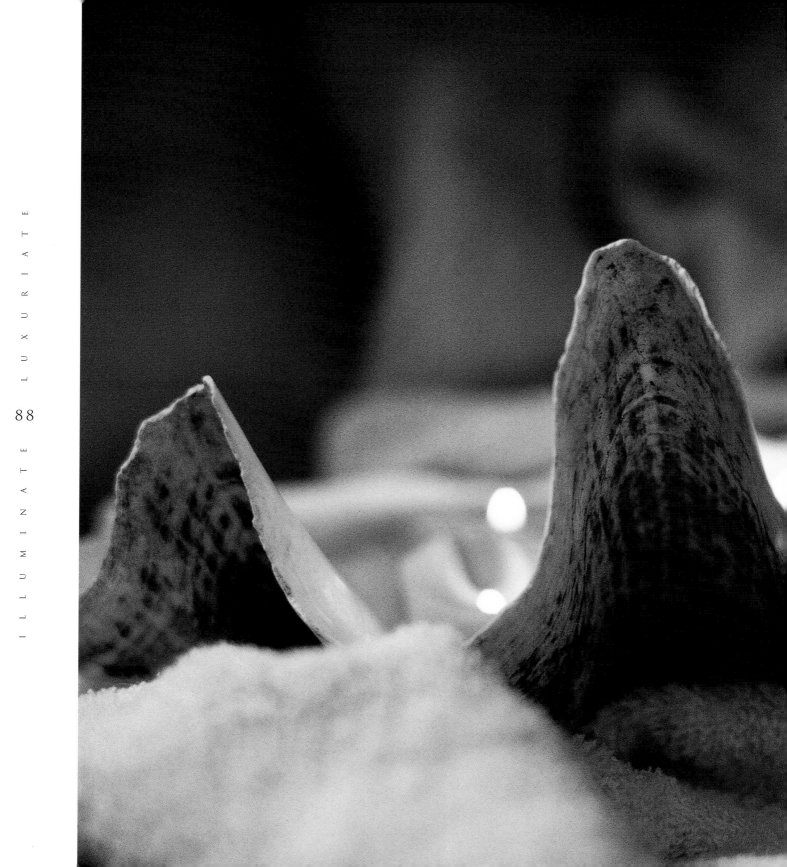

If you are entertaining and want to treat guests to a candle-lit bathroom, be sure to select candles that are safe to leave unattended for a few hours. A shallow bowl of scented, floating candles by the hand basin or at the end of the bath creates a sensual mood. Find accessories that add a sense of LUXURY, such as this clamshell. Look for antique trays, punchbowls, and one-of-a-kind lead crystal goblets.

Pile on the GLAMOUR
with this luxurious project. You will
need a heat-safe glass and a handful
of clean feathers. Feathers can be
found in craft stores. Or buy a section
of boa and carefully remove the
longer intact feathers.

1 Although a petite example is shown here, a larger project using a vase and peacock feathers, or raven's quills, would be quite spectacular.

2 Using a tube of superglue with an applicator, apply a fine line of glue around the perimeter of the glass, about 1 inch (2.5 cm) from the base.

3 Working quickly before the glue dries, stick each feather around the glass, each quill toward the base. When fully dry, place a candle in the glass.

4 This ultraluxurious votive will create a heavenly bedside glow, a much softer alternative to overhead lighting when a romantic atmosphere is desired.

WITH THE TURNING OF
THE SEASONS,

the air chills, the wind whips the last of the leaves from the trees, winter arrives, and so does the instinct to hibernate. Whether you are snowed in or just want to keep the frost from your door, winter is the perfect time to spend by the hearth at home. Winter evokes the thought of open fires, tea and toast, big

fluffy sweaters, and cozy rooms filled with the scent of PINE, CINNAMON, and CHOCOLATE. Colors change from the golden tones of autumn to the colder hues of winter and shorter days make for sharp shadows. While some shiver, waiting for the arrival of spring, others give themselves over to the season and embrace all that winter brings.

A time for reflection, drawing in, and closing down, winter is a vital part of the cycle of life where fishermen mend their nets and the world rests for a while. Animals hibernate, sleeping snugly through the coldest months and living off the fat of their bodies till spring. Humans are drawn to heat and comfort where fire replaces the sun with golden flames and warmth, and candles grace our mantlepieces. A preoccupation with keeping warm dictates our clothes, our décor, and our choice of food. Cold weather calls for cheerful entertaining. Guests need to feel bolstered and nurtured, so consider warmth and comfort by using earthy tones, responsive textures, familiar fragrances, and comfort food, such as hearty casseroles, bread pudding, and decanters of plummy red wine. Observe nature for decorating clues.

Pick a palette of winter colors that are rosy and delicious. RUST, DEEP CHOCOLATE, and BRONZE are all harmonious and classic. Grays need to be given a nudge of berry red or burnt orange to transform them into a welcoming friend.

As the focus in winter is on being indoors, it is a good idea to create a variety of lifestyle spaces to alleviate boredom and allow for friends and family to experience an interlude of rest and fresh inspiration. A covered veranda can be armed with deep, snug chairs, and plush rugs for rain watching. Sheltered spots in the garden can be used to catch a few rays of winter sun, and humble corners can be instantly transformed into cozy nests with the addition of an old rocking chair, soft woolly blankets, and a stash of must-read books.

Candles take center stage when it is cold, adorning our mantles and hearths. Just as we warm to firelight, a flame is a compelling focal point. When the days are long and dark, candles can be ablaze throughout the day, adding romance and festivity to what otherwise could be a bleak and gray outlook. Put sumptuous scents to work by placing perfumed candles in unexpected places. ORANGE, TANGERINE, and BERGAMOT lift the spirits, while ginger, cypress, and eucalyptus purify the air to keep colds and flu at bay. LEMON, BASIL, and SPRUCE provide subtle inspiration, if all you want to do is roll over and snuggle back down.

TEXTURE plays a vital role here, with rough wooden plates and seasonal finds from the garden, such as pine cones and needles, providing a scented nest. The candles, having a solid shape, work well as a single display or when grouped as a set. Create rustic displays by hunting for objects reminiscent of woodlands and forests. This idea is very effective as a table arrangement—try a long wooden tray with candles in a line.

Be greeted by a familiar FRAGRANCE. Candles infused with cinnamon, vanilla, spice, mulled wine, and chocolate, can be positioned at floor level along the hallway for a beautiful and welcoming light. By creating a pathway to follow, guests are steered toward the living room for predinner drinks, then on to the dining room for a formal meal.

Take inspiration from the rich palette of "drawing room" colors—old chocolate leather, lush cream, and red velvets.

TRADITIONAL

Persian rugs, English tapestries, and well-worn mahogany woods add charm to the surroundings. By using candles instead of traditional lighting, the room takes on a whole new character. Even with less formal décor, place a sofa right by the bookcase where it will lure you to browse, time and time again, through your literary collection. Have a chess set, port, and a stash of homemade rum candies on hand, and convert your drawing room into a gentleman's club.

99

Whether you choose oversized, roughly woven ethnic panniers or a demure tray like this one, baskets are the ideal WINTER accessory. Mobile and easily stashed, they create anything from a mini-fireplace effect to a series of tiny twinkling baskets. We lined this basket with heat resistant fabric and ensured that the candles were secure and away from the handle.

Fend off the winter chill with a luxurious quilt or throw and VELVETY cushions on your favorite chaise longue. A cross between a couch and a bed, the chaise longue is the ultimate winter perch. Add a romantic novel, snuggle up to a hot-water bottle, and hibernate. Central areas of light are easily added to any location by clustering candles together to add warmth to cold corners, or extra coziness to a favorite nook.

A MAGICAL highlight
to winter entertaining is a pathway of
flickering candles on chilly nights.
Cold stone steps are instantly warmed,
and the night is transformed with the
aroma of amber, frankincense, and
myrrh. To recreate the effect, fill deep
terra-cotta or stone pots with solid
candles and tie autumnal leaves,
berries, and twigs to the bases.

102

Due to the size of the wick,
OUTDOOR candles
will withstand rain, hail, sleet, and snow.
These candles have wicks made of 100
percent cotton window sash to ensure
they will light up and stay ablaze in the
most inclement weather. Rough brown
paper has been tied around this pot,
well away from the flame, as a ready gift
for a keen gardener.

This pair of oversized candles was custom-made for the household to create a grand, ILLUMINATING entrance to the doorway. Guests adore the warm winter glow and are enchanted by their unusual shape, and the bare branches set into the exterior ring of the wax (safely away from flame). A local chandler should be able to make custom candles for your needs, particularly if you have an area that needs a vibrant living light. Of course, it is even more rewarding to create unique candles yourself.

This candle was richly scented with the seasonal SPICES of bayberry, myrrh, nutmeg, and vanilla, creating the delicious aroma of plum pudding.

Adding to the WARMTH of the occasion, candles in the colors of pomegranate, stone, bronze, cinnamon, and chocolate are rich and welcoming. The evening has been given a formal touch by using tiebacks with the curtains to create a theatrical entrance. Guests can peek at the preparations of the feast within, while sipping mulled wine on the large wooden veranda. Within the room, golden light radiates from several spots, allowing guests to see that chaise longues are draped with velvet and fur throws for after-dinner lazing. The rich cinnamon scent from the candles and the cozy warmth of the open log fire beckon all indoors, leaving the winter chill outside.

The formality of this room is RELAXED by a table setting of clustered candles and fruit. An antique cast-iron urn creates a robust centerpiece. Fresh ivy has been wrapped around bare branches, then spice-scented tealights are hung from little wire lanterns in the branches. Reminiscent of a harvest festival supper, the use of natural decorations in the stunning golden tones of autumn creates an unmistakable seasonal flavor.

A timeless and FESTIVE cornucopia. Set your table to reflect the feel of an Old Master's still life painting by using a panoply of apples, tamarillos, pears, and berries, or a bowl brimming with ripe lemons and leaves as your centerpiece. Candles are both square and round with different heights and colors to provide many levels of light. A subtle injection of navy and old gold adds to the overall richness, as does a scattering of nuts and berries. Sheaves of wheat, pumpkins, and tiny bunches of ruby red grapes can also be included.

Hunt for candles and accessories that reflect the mood of the SEASON. Seek traditional ideas from older relations and books that recount rituals from the past. In times gone by, oranges were studded with cloves and rolled in nutmeg and orris root to preserve them, then they were hung by the fireside to freshen the air and to generate good cheer. Little did our forebears know that this was an effective aromatherapy treatment to ward away colds and lift the spirits. Contemporary cheer comes from this candle which is bursting with orange, cinnamon, and clove.

WEEKENDS are a time to putter around wrapped in shawls until the morning chill has lifted. Shawls and pashminas offer practical warmth, as they can double as throws and blankets. Feast on big bowls of oatmeal with cream and brown sugar, and sip freshly-brewed coffee. Winter storms mean the fire is kept burning all day. Throw some orange peel into the flames to revive the stuffy atmosphere—the scent of orange is uplifting and cheering.

112

Take a moment to watch the winter wildlife in the GARDEN from the shelter of a wide veranda. A lovely rocking chair and garden bench create a secluded retreat. Add the glow of candles, a soft throw, and a hot cup of tea. The pages of an old children's storybook have been used as lantern shades for basic white candles. Fireproofing paper and parchment is easily done by painting with flame retardant and allowing to dry, then tying string around a candle to form a hurricane lamp effect. Pages from used art books, children's paintings, magazines, and greeting cards can all be used for a similar effect.

There is something romantic about creating an outdoor library for the day— particularly if you stack your new reading room with velvet throws in rich, dramatic colors. An old, RUSTIC droplight from a barn has been refitted with candles. Take this theme to the extreme and create a dinner party under the winter stars. Warm the evening with braziers and light the occasion with chandeliers filled with creamy wax.

For this effect buy a plain spicy scented candle in a RICH color, such as bronze. The size of the candle is important as it must be about the same height as a cinnamon stick— and wide enough in circumference to avoid the sticks catching alight from the lit flame. Cinnamon sticks are available from the spice section of the local supermarket and 3 feet (1m) of fine leather thonging can be purchased from a shoe repair store.

114

1

2

1 Cut the cinnamon sticks to the same length.

2 Tie the fine leather thonging continuously around each individual cinnamon stick.

3 Before tying them to the candle, sprinkle the sticks with fragrant oil such as pine, frankincense, or myrrh. To ensure the garland does not slip off, press a few straight sewing pins into the candle.

4 For a beautiful warming winter glow, arrange a set of rustic cinnamon candles next to each other, adding sensuality to a stark winter garden.

RATE

CELEBRATIONS PUNCTUATE THE RHYTHM OF OUR WORLD,

they mark the changing seasons, the passage of time, and the coming together of life and love. On these occasions there is a need to break bread together, share memories, moments, and laughter, connect with those we love, and take stock and give thanks. It's a time to express excitement, joy, and friendship.

Celebration and feasting go hand-in-hand. The ancient art of feasting signified abundance and indulgence, and was often accompanied by "killing a fatted calf"—a custom to share joy in the form of rich food with as many people as possible. In contemporary times, this level of excess is more symbolic, with a successful celebration dependent on capturing a special SPIRIT or EMOTION. These are the celebrations where imagination and creativity combine with warmth and generosity to create a certain "magic."

Taking the time to add final touches and details to a celebration is a reemerging art form. They say "God is in the details" so, having less time to dispose of, the modern host or hostess focuses on simple fuss-free food, creating a memorable ambience, and saving enough energy to enjoy a sparkling conversation. Entertaining is one of the best ways to celebrate your own personal style. Whether you are opening your home to friends for dinner, or having the whole family over for Christmas Day, it's important to make your guests feel at home without turning your life upside down. The key to effortless entertaining is a solid theme and keeping it simple. Ensure your home feels comfortable and conversation will flow naturally.

Place small twinkling lights in nooks and crannies—consider all the available surfaces as potential candle homes—and surprise your guests. Frame your front door with an archway of candles to create a grand entrance. Create avenues of light at floor level, along corridors, and on stairs to lead guests along magical pathways that beg to be explored. Treat guests to a bathroom full of scented, flickering candles so that the mood of your celebration flows from room to room.

Embellishments don't need to cost a fortune. Consider what resources you have on hand and don't be shy about experimenting with new looks or themes that excite you. For example, if you have a tree with large leaves in your garden, use the foliage to create a tablecloth for an authentic twist to a curry or spicy meal. A table setting need not be conservative or predictable. Combine flowers, petals, and candles for a simple yet stylish means of decoration. Use candles of varying heights to create interest or scatter bright festive touches such as GLITTER, STARS, FEATHERS, and CRYSTALS around the base of candle clusters to reflect the light and attract the eye. Coordinate the décor with the menu you have selected to create the right mood, imbuing a sense of harmony that flows through to the food and wine. Whatever theme you choose, make a statement, be generous, and be sure that you share the whole experience with the people you love.

Chic and SIMPLE, a theme of silver and arctic white gives this table a timeless elegance. Although the lines and decorations are kept clean, by injecting a few whimsical touches such as silver candy balls and sparklers, the mood suddenly takes on a more celebratory air. By bringing carefully selected props into play, guests do not have to compete to shine—rather they add the vital element—good fun and laughter.

When planning a celebration theme, don't underestimate the importance of carrying the look through to your chairs. For more formal functions, streamlined contemporary furniture can be softened, but not obscured, with translucent cotton. Generous back panels have been sewn to these slipcovers and the hems drawn together with fine silver cord and finished with silver baubles and hand-made CRYSTAL beads to add elegance to the scene. Trimming with pretty white flowers such as gardenias or daisies will give the setting a more romantic finish. Equally, quirky trims such as antique and pearl silverware, costume jewels, or Christmas decorations will give strong direction to your table concept.

Silver and white is a classic color combination that can be translated to any occasion. White is the neutral that provides a gracious backdrop. Silver, like gold, is a statement—rich, SPARKLING, and full of pizazz. This dining room is in a large innercity apartment that is a converted warehouse. To make the celebration more intimate, the table has been moved to a corner and screened to create a warmer atmosphere for a gathering of six.

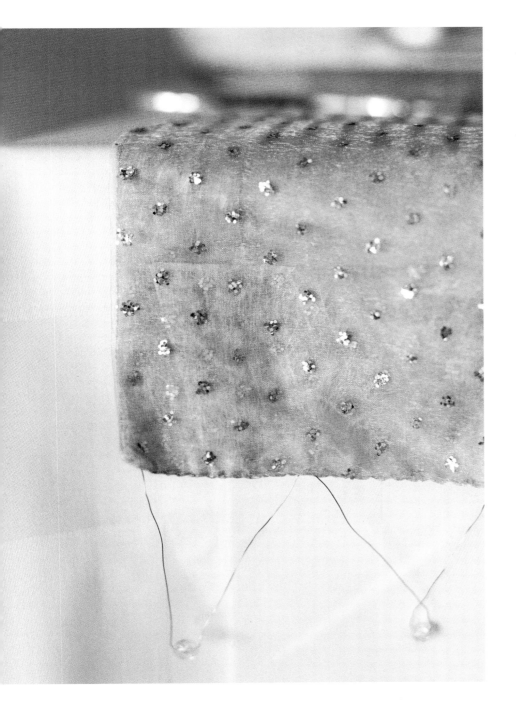

Starry, STARRY night.
The focus will always go to where the light is, so use this to your advantage. Menus, seating arrangements, and instructions can be subtly highlighted for guests on arrival with a strategically placed candle.

Sheer and beaded fabrics provide a
DAZZLING party
sparkle, with some of the best effects achieved by layering. Whether they are hung from the ceiling as a screen to divide a room, or simply used to give a diaphanous, summery feel to the table, most fabrics can bring a soft airiness to hard-edged interiors. This runner has been layered onto a linen tablecloth and given a wire and bead trim for weight.

Personal touches make guests feel especially welcome. Here, entrée plates hold silver stars, glass prisms, and foil garden tags EMBELLISHED with a tassel. Place cards offer an excellent opportunity to highlight a theme. They also allow the host to strategically place diners in the best possible way to ensure bright conversation. Display names on unexpected everyday objects such as eggs, or carve them into softer objects like driftwood. Spell initials using sprinkles or colored sugar on cupcakes, or use old childhood photographs if it's a family function. For corporate events, have fun with the obvious—computer companies could have an apple at each place spiked with a cocktail flag. Among the endless possibilities for creative place cards, work with the fun and surreal to thrill even the most jaded dinner guest.

Here, fragile wax cups were hand formed to provide the most DELICATE glow. Recreate this look by sourcing lightweight paper cups, hand-ripping the tops to make an irregular lip, and pretreating with flame retardant. Place a small candle inside. Guests' names, messages, poems, or patterns can be drawn or punctured into the cups using a fine needle. If the paper cups have a wax coating, as many do, pressed flowers, decorative paper, and fine cord can be carefully dry ironed onto the surface. Protect the surface of the iron with a piece of thick brown paper, and be sure to use the lowest heat setting.

125

Candles do not always have to be lit to be STRIKING. These retro-style silver beads are tied by a fine silver cord to the wick to carry the theme through. Feathers, stars, tassels, or crystals can also be used to create a similar effect.

126

Reassess old traditions and have fun
creating new ones. Here, the usual
floral decorations are replaced with
a low bowl piled with rock-candy
sugar and SILVER balls,
accentuated by a tiny
flickering candle.

SHINING simplicity!
Wrap metallic elastic around a wide
candle, tucking in little stars as you go.
A group of candles that has received
this treatment looks superb, particularly
if you select candles of varying heights
in shades of white and gray. Even
humble household tapers can be
transformed in this way, bringing a
celebratory twist to any occasion.

Vases of all types can double as candleholders. Here, fine tapers have been
CLUSTERED
into a bed of silver stars. A cup filled
with ice, sugar cubes, granulated sugar,
or rock salt is another alternative
base for candles to sit in.

With a twist of silver cardboard
and some carefully placed pins, uplights are
devised to make enchanting lamps on the table.
Be sure to keep untreated paper well away from
the flame. Use small glass votives if you're unsure.
SOPHISTICATED party
favors for grownups take
the form of mini-organza bags
filled with tiny silver stars—a treat
for guests to play with.

Introduce a second dimension of
table lighting, with smaller candles
dotted among the larger ones. These
little lanterns are easily constructed
by pinning a section of stiff, sheer
ribbon to the metallic casing on
tealights. Diffused low lights are more
personal and add a touch of warmth
and INTIMACY.

Fire and ice. A customized candle is shaped like a serving tray to present FRESHLY shucked oysters. Made in a size that is manageable to hand around to guests, this centerpiece functions as a platter, icebox, and candle.

Quirky ideas with ice and wax sculptures will always inject DRAMA, individuality, and a sense of theater into any special occasion.

134

Adjusting the lighting in each entertaining area, along with fragrances and soft music, will enable the FESTIVE mood and conversation to continue from beginning to end. Start the evening with scented candles or an aromatherapy blend that is relaxing and congenial. Lemon verbena, spearmint, lavender, geranium, and neroli are excellent fragrances for this. Lemon, lime, basil, rosemary, tangerine, and sandalwood are the least imposing when eating. Stronger perfumes are not always welcome with food, as they compete with the flavors. After the main meal, the deeper sensual fragrances of rose, patchouli, frankincense, cedarwood, vanilla, and jasmine are a real pleasure. When using essential oils, never use more than six drops in an oil burner. When blending oils or bringing together scented candles, limit your choice to a mix of three perfumes. This allows the blend to be interesting without becoming confused.

Set against an iridescent backdrop, the colors and textures of
the food become star attractions. Consider how your food can
HARMONIZE or contrast with colors in a setting,
and again with the color scheme of your tableware. As a guide,
savory flavors are more appetizing presented on dramatic
contrasting colors, while sweet or delicate flavors do well
with a softer harmonizing palette.

You are never too old to enjoy the thrill of playing with a
SPARKLER—arguably the quickest, easiest, and most cost-effective way of throwing an instant party. Guests can be handed sparklers along with their slices of cake and asked to conduct one another in a chorus of song.

136

A stylized treat for the absolute
MINIMALIST!
A cheeky presentation of birthday candles is welcome for those who cannot, or wish not, to eat cake.

A lighthearted cake is a
FUN contrast to the formality of the solid silver tableware. When diners retire to the sofa, the candelabra is placed at the rear of the table, rather than in its usual central position, creating a delightful ceremonial backdrop.

Add to a CHIC white-on-white theme by embellishing plain candles with a shimmering twist. You will need white candles, liquid glue, a paintbrush, and aluminum foil.

1 Metallic candles are often difficult to find and the designs can be limiting. Create your own easily and inexpensively. Start by selecting a trio of white candles in various heights.

2 Decide on a pattern or design for the foil. Paint a thin coat of liquid glue on the surface of the candle in the areas you wish to be covered in silver. We chose a rough "landscape" design.

3 Cut or rip the foil into sections and place on the candle in your desired design. Rub the foil firmly down on the glued surface, smoothing out any wrinkles or trapped air bubbles. Allow to dry.

4 The result is a simple yet effective look, ideal for any celebration.

CANDLES ARE LIVING LIGHTS...

With so many possibilities on the market today, it is possible to buy virtually any shape, color, style, or size of candle you desire. Making a superb gift, candles are a popular choice for presents on any occasion. Whatever your reason for welcoming a candle into your home, selection can be assisted by following a few simple rules:

- Consider if the candle requires a special holder.
- Find a manufacturer that sells high-quality candles. Usually the best are handmade. Check whether the candles are made from food-grade paraffin wax, which is the best material for burning.
- Generally, you get what you pay for. A low-quality candle is inexpensive and will not burn well or last very long. A good quality candle is an investment and should be chosen carefully as it will be burning for many hundreds of hours.
- Not all candles are fragrant. Unscented candles are best used at the dining table so they don't compete with the flavors of the food.
- Candles should come with a care label or instructions. Look for reputable manufacturers who offer a contact telephone number.
- Refer to the wick guide on this page and ensure that the size of the wick in the candle you are buying is suitable for the location.

TECHNICAL INFORMATION

All candles share two things—wick and wax. Candlelight is generated when wax is melted by the heat of a flame and is drawn up the wick by capillary action. Waxes are a complex mixture of esters, fatty acids, alcohol, and hydrocarbons. This allows for slow, steady, and complete combustion—unlike wood, for example, which leaves ash behind.

Today's commercially available candles are primarily made from paraffin wax—a fast-burning white material which is a by-product of petroleum and other hydrocarbons. This wax comes in various qualities based on the extent of the refining process. Beeswax, canuba, and palm oil are frequently used as mixers to make candles burn longer. Scents, colors, and additives are also added to the mix. Candle making is very much like cooking, and every chef has a different recipe depending on the blend of waxes, oils, and colors used. A far cry from the primitive wicks that were once made from branches dipped in animal fat, today's wicks are braided, woven, or twisted lengths of cord, usually made from soft cotton. The thickness of the wick remains crucial to performance. Too much wick means a larger flame, creating too much heat which can melt through the candle walls.

THE WICK

It is vital that the correct wick has been chosen for the candle. Factors include the size of the candle and the blend of waxes that has been used. If the wick is too long or thick, it will burn and smoke. If the wick is too short or thin, the resulting flame will be very small and it will drown. It isn't the actual wick that burns—the wick just links the vapor from the molten wax to the flame—it is the vapor that burns as the fuel is drawn up the wick. The most popular wicks are made from flat braided cotton and have been dipped in a waxy solution to retard the burning. This process is called "priming."

OUTDOOR WICK—Extremely thick braided cotton that will withstand strong breezes. The thickness can range from $\frac{1}{4}$ to $\frac{1}{2}$ inch (5–12 mm).

COURTYARD WICK—Medium-sized, braided wick, from $\frac{1}{8}$ to $\frac{1}{4}$ inch (3–5 mm) in thickness.

INDOOR WICK—Finely braided cotton wicking ranging from $\frac{1}{2}$ to $\frac{1}{8}$ inch (1–3 mm) in thickness.

MULTIWICK—A candle that has more than one wick.

METAL WICK—Has a fine wire woven within the cotton wick, causing it to stay upright independently. Mainly used in container candles where the majority of fuel or wax becomes liquid. Of recent times, there has been concern that inferior metal wicks contain lead, which is highly poisonous. Check at time of purchase that the seller is aware of this problem and does not stock lead wick products.

COMMERCIAL CANDLE SHAPES

CONTAINER—Any candle that is poured into a vessel and is burned in that vessel.

PILLAR—A thick, freestanding candle.

VOTIVE—A glass in which to place a tealight, or a glass partially filled with soft wax.

MOLDED—Novelty shapes.

TAPER—Long, thin cylindrical candles.

DANISH TAPERS—Very thin tapers.

TEALIGHTS—Small metal container filled with wax.

FLOATING CANDLES—Candles designed to float in water.

SCULPTURAL—Big feature candles, usually too large for tabletops, that rest on the floor.

HONEYCOMB SHEETS—Wax honeycomb sheets rolled around a wick to create a simple candle.

SCENTED CANDLES

Mood enhancing, intoxicating, and romantic, the allure of scented candles is irresistible. The degree to which we can smell the aroma of scented candles is affected by a number of factors:

- The specific fragrance—some scents are quite simply stronger.
- The size of the room—a smaller room will contain the fragrant vapor in a higher concentration creating a stronger impression.
- Air flow and quality—since fragrant vapor is carried in the air, factors such as humidity, air conditioning, fans, and open windows, will affect its movement.
- The size of the wax pool—the greater the surface of liquid wax, the more the fragrance will evaporate into the air.
- The size of the flame—a large flame will burn more of the fragrant vapor before it can escape into the air (keep the wick trimmed).
- The temperature at which a fragrance is vaporized—some vaporize more readily, permeating the air to a greater extent.
- Length of exposure—our nose desensitizes to fragrances over time.

What is the difference between a fragrance or perfume and an essential oil?

An essential oil is a volatile oil, extracted from a natural botanical source. Essential oils have a genuine therapeutic benefit and are costly. Their delicate chemicals make them sensitive to extreme heat—a clumsy choice for use in candles as the fragrant molecules tend to evaporate during the manufacturing process. Nevertheless, pure oils do get used in candles by specialty manufacturers, who have perfected techniques to harness the beauty of essential oil.

Perfumes, fragrances, or scents, as they are sometimes known, are man-made. Manufactured in laboratories, they can be engineered to withstand the rigors of the manufacturing process. Many scents that do not naturally occur in nature, or are impossible to capture, can be magically produced in a test tube. For example berry, grass, and pear do not have enough volatile oils to be captured naturally, so a chemist recreates an impression artificially. For flowers and fruits that are rare, this is wonderful technology as it allows popular fragrances such as vanilla to be produced in huge quantities for a reasonable price.

SCENTED CANDLE GUIDE

WELCOMING SCENTS—Robust warm fragrances, coffee, nuts, vanilla, cinnamon, nutmeg, orange, apple, berry scents, patchouli, vetiver, and clove.

RELAXING SCENTS—Light florals or fruits and gentle herbaceous scents, chamomile, hops, jasmine, linden, clary sage, and peach.

INVIGORATING SCENTS—Marine and oceanic types, mountain air scents, gutsy herbaceous aromas, licorice, basil, bay, cedarwood, grapefruit, lemon, peppermint, pine, and rosemary.

APHRODISIACS—Musky oriental aromas, rich woods, spices, deep orchid scents, cardamom, coriander, ginger, narcissus, ylang ylang, and rose.

BALANCING SCENTS—Woodland scents, grassy and hay scents, moss, leaf and forest scents, bergamot, geranium, lavender, and neroli.

COMMON CHEMICAL ADDITIVES AND INGREDIENTS

Paraffin wax is the most basic candle ingredient. It is a by-product of the oil industry, produced by the refining of crude oil. Paraffin wax is odorless and colorless, and is mainly available in pellet form. When the wax has melted, the result is a transparent thin liquid that looks like water. As the wax cools it starts to solidify. Paraffin wax has a wide melting range between 104–160° F (40–70° C). The melting point is a factor in how rapidly the candle burns—a low melting temperature causes the candle to burn faster.

BEESWAX—This is one of the oldest candle-making materials known to humans. It has a wonderful perfume and texture, and comes in many different variations of its natural color—from light yellow to deep brown. It is also available in a bleached white form. Small amounts of beeswax are still added to many candles to increase the burn time. An average addition is 25 percent. Beeswax melts to a syrupy consistency and becomes very sticky.

SASSOL—A manufacturing aid. This chemical contributes to the sharpness of shape in a mold. For instance, it is used to achieve very sharp corners and a crisp finish on square candles.

VYBAR—Adds viscosity to wax.

DYES—Add color to candles and are designed to be soluble in wax.

ULTRAVIOLET FILTERS—Prevent candle dye from fading in sunlight.

STEARIC ACID—Stearic acid is used with paraffin to reduce its tendency to shrink, which is helpful to manufac-turers. It also helps give a good color and stops the candle from dripping.

METHODS OF CANDLE PRODUCTION

DIPPED—These candles are made by repeatedly dipping a piece of wick into melted wax contained in a dipping can.

DRAWN—This is an old method made new by modern technology. It involves pulling lengths of wick through melted wax. This method works for making small diameter candles such as birthday candles, or the long waxed wicks called lighting tapers.

EXTRUDED—This is a machine method that pushes wax out through a shaped template or dye.

POURED—Refers to an old-fashioned method of pouring wax into a mold. It is labor intensive, but produces candles of the most superior quality.

PRESSED—This is a newer method of making commercial candles in which wax is atomized into a cooling drum, forming wax beads and granules. These beads are then compressed into molds, where they bind to form a candle. They are quick, cheap, and easy to produce. The drawback is the poor quality and low burning time.

ROLLED—These candles are made by rolling sheets of wax around the wick. Tapers, pillars, and novelty candles can be made by this method.

SAND-MOLD—Wet sand can been used to create a free-form mold.

CANDLE HOLDERS

LANTERNS AND LAMPS—Have a base and walls to protect the candle feom being blown out.

CANDLESTICKS—Vertical holders with prickets or cups to stabilize a candle.

CANDELABRA—Holders with a number of arms each finished with a pricket and plate to prevent dripping.

SCONCE—A wall panel with holders.

CHANDELIER—A crown of holders designed to hang from the ceiling.

ACCESSORIES

SHADE—Much like a lampshade, shades are usually constructed from inflammable material to fit over a candle and create a softer light.

DRIP CATCHER—Little plate to protect surfaces from wax drips.

WICK TRIMMER—Small sharp scissors with a box to collect spent wicks.

CANDLE BOX—Storage box hung on the wall.

CHRISTMAS TREE HOLDER—Small metallic grip, similar to a clothes peg, which clips on branches. A miniature cup allows tiny candles to be inserted into the clip.

SNUFFER—Cone attached to a handle that fits over the flame to snuff it out and reduce smoke. Use of a snuffer also prevents the candle splashing, which can occur when blowing it out.

CANDLE STICKIES—Commercially produced dots of malleable tack, to keep a candle in place within its holder.

CANDLE CARE & SAFETY

A little bit of care goes a long way toward keeping a candle burning beautifully and safely.

- Never leave a burning candle unattended.
- Keep wicks trimmed to ⅛–¼ inch (5 mm) long as crooked wicks can cause uneven burning and dripping.
- If the tip of the wick has curled to one side during burning it has burned for too long.
- When first burning a pillar, allow the

wax to pool to ½ inch (1 cm) of the outside edge. Extinguish and let wax harden before relighting. You will find that the candle then has a "memory" and will not burn past this point again. It has formed a barrier.

- A general rule is to burn candles for one hour per each inch (2.5 cm) of diameter every time you light it. The flame needs time to soften and melt the wax to the outer edge. Burning for less time will cause the candle to bore a hole down the middle resulting in drowned wicks.
- Occasionally rotate the candle. This will assist in even burning.
- Do not allow wick trimmings, matches, or other debris to remain in the wax pool as they can ignite.
- Never place a burning candle in a draft as this causes uneven burning and excessive dripping.
- Always burn candles on a protected heat-resistant surface.
- The surface should be solid and sturdy to prevent the candle from falling over.
- Burn candles away from flammable soft furnishings.
- Do not burn candles in small, enclosed spaces, such as a bookshelf or under shelves.
- Use caution when extinguishing candles. Do not pour water over them and be aware of the wax pool "splashing" when blowing them out. Snuff candles out in preference to blowing them out.
- Keep the burning wick upright and central. If it is drooping to one side, snuff out the candle, trim the wick and use an object such as tweezers or a metal skewer to recenter the wick.
- Keep burning candles away from children and animals.
- Snuff candles out and wait until the wax hardens before moving them.
- Display and store candles away from direct light—they fade when exposed to bright light for extended lengths of time.
- Before you entertain, light and extinguish candles—they will light more easily later on.
- If burning more than one candle at a time, especially pillars, arrange them a minimum of 2 inches (5 cm) apart for proper burning.
- Always secure tapers into their holders. Sticky gum works well.

WHAT AFFECTS THE BURN RATE?

- The temperature of the day. Cool wax burns longer than warm wax.
- If candles are stored in a refrigerator's freezing compartment, you will get a slightly longer burning time—however if the temperature change is too dramatic, you may get cracks in the candle called "thermo shock."
- Different types of wax have different burning times.
- Color, fragrance, and specific usage affect wax consumption.
- Wick size.
- The diameter of the candle.

CANDLE STORAGE

- Store in a cool, dark, dry place.

- Store tapers flat to prevent warping.
- If candles are being stored in a damp area, seal them in foil or an airtight container to prevent the wick from becoming moldy or moist.
- Replace the lid (if supplied) on scented candles when not being burned. This will help the candles retain their fragrance.

CLEANING TIPS

- To keep a candle looking glossy and new, gently rub its surface with old pantyhose.
- Add a teaspoon of water to the bottom of a tealight holder to make it easier to clean.
- Do not display candles in overly sunny areas, such as windows. This may cause the dye to fade and the candle to melt.

CANDLE CLEAN UP

Many candle manufacturers sell products for cleaning wax spills, however there are other simple cleaning methods available. Always use hot water with caution when dissolving wax. Do not allow any waxy water to go down the drain because it can clog the plumbing. It is best to pour the waxy water into a container for garbage disposal. Brightly colored wax, which may hold a great deal of dye in it, could impregnate porous materials, and may require two phases of cleaning—first to remove the wax, and secondly to remove the dye stain.

METHODS OF WAX REMOVAL

FREEZE AND CHIP
Place object in the freezer until wax becomes very brittle. The wax will chip away easily without residue. This method is suitable for metal objects and plastics.

IRONING WITH BROWN PAPER
Best if wax has penetrated the fibers of fabric. Place brown paper over the wax and iron at a medium heat. The wax will transfer to the paper—you may need to do this a few times. Professional carpet cleaning is recommended for heavily soiled wax spills on rugs and carpets.

POWDERED SOAP AND A LITTLE HOT WATER
Remove the bulk of the wax very carefully with a knife. Use hot water. This method is suitable for fabrics and removing smoke stains from walls.

WALLS WITH DRY SOOT DAMAGE
Sponge down walls with dry soot damage. Then wipe walls over with a little white spirit.

WHITE SPIRIT
This chemical is similar to that used by dry cleaners and is usually available in small amounts from hardware stores. Dissolves wax readily from most fabrics. It is highly flammable so follow directions carefully.

U.S. SUPPLIERS

CANDLES AND ACCESSORIES
The Candle Barn
(973) 243-0697
www.thecandlebarn.com

Candle Cents
1-888-336-3915
www.candlecents.com

Candlemart
1-877-352-6353
www.candlemart.com

The Candlestick
1-800-972-6777
www.thecandlestick.com

Cierra Candles
1-800-281-4337
www.cierracandles.com

Creative Candles
1-800-237-9711
www.creativecandles.com

General Wax Co.
1-800-929-7867
www.genwax.com

Illuminations
1-800-CANDLES
www.illuminations.com

Knorr Candle Factory and Shop
(858) 755-2051
www.knorrcandleshop.com

Meyralights (smokeless/dripless)
(206) 633-1284
www.meyralights.com

The Wax House Corp.
1-888-WAX-9711
www.waxhouse.com

The White Barn Candle Company
(Throughout U.S.)
www.whitebarncandle.com

Wicks' End
1-800-WICKS-END
www.wicksend.com

Wicks 'n' Sticks
1-888-55-WICKS
www.wicksnsticks.com

FIRE-RETARDANT PRODUCTS FOR USE IN CRAFTING CANDLEHOLDERS
Flame Seal Products, Inc.
(713) 668-4291
www.flameseal.com

National Fireproofing Company
1-888-391-3981
www.natfire.com

FSI
1-800-227-2694
www.fireprevention.com